MOON SWALLOWER

A PLAY BY
Colby Quick

MOON SWALLOWER

A PLAY BY

Colby Quick

The Play Right Series

MOON SWALLOWER
Copyright 2022 by Colby Quick.
All rights reserved.
Printed in the United States of America. No parts of this publication may be reproduced in any manner without written permission except in the case of brief quotations embodied in critical analyses and reviews.

Library of Congress Number: 2022942968

ISBN: 978-1-942081-31-9
A publication of The Jasper Project, Chapin, South Carolina

Cover Art by Julie Schuler

The Play Right Series

JasperProject.Org

The Play Right Series

The purpose of the Jasper Project's Play Right Series is to:

Empower and enlighten audiences by allowing them insider views of the processes of creating theatre art;

Increase opportunities for theatre artists to create and participate in new art without the necessity of being attached to an existing theatre organization; and to

Provide more affordable and experimental theatre arts experiences for new and emerging theatre artists and their audiences; thereby expanding cultural literacy and theatre arts appreciation in the South Carolina Midlands.

FOREWORD

What we've got here is something new under the sun.

This book is the first of many, one hopes, to emerge from The Jasper Project's Play Right Series, whose goal is to cultivate a larger, more cohesive community of theater practitioners and consumers in the midlands and, best of all, if you ask me, to create more opportunities for plays and playwrights.

It works like this: South Carolina playwrights—those living in or native to the state—are invited to submit previously unproduced one-act plays. One play is selected for a several-month development cycle culminating in a rehearsed, public stage-reading. The development cycle consists of readings and discussions with actors, technicians, literary types and Community Producers—persons wanting to venture beyond the veil of the production process and get involved in the creation of each new play. Community Producers attend and participate at table readings, rehearsals, and conversations with the cast, director, costumers, stage manager, etc.

The Jasper Project wishes to thank, truly and madly and deeply, this year's Community Producers for making this series and indeed this book possible. They are Bert Easter, Ed Madden, James Smith, Kirkland Smith, Bill Schmidt, Paul Leo, Eric Tucker, Cindi Boiter, and Wade Sellers.

The first play selected for the Play Right Series, in 2017, was *Sharks and Other Lovers*, by Randall David Cook. After its PRS debut, Randall's play went on to full production, as the winner of its New Play Festival, at Greenville's Centre Stage theatre. Now The Jasper Project has teamed with Muddy Ford Press to make permanent, via publication, each year's chosen play.

You're holding this year's: Colby Quick's *Moon Swallower*. Colby describes his play's genesis in the Preface to follow, and after that, the play will speak quite assuredly for itself, so I won't say much here.

Except this: you've never read anything like it. You've never read a more poignant domestic comedy triangulating YouTube, addiction and lycanthropy. What we've got here is a new voice, one worth listening to.

Enjoy.

- Jon Tuttle

August 2022

PREFACE

I grew up watching horror movies with my family and still obsess over them today, especially films from the '80s like *Evil Dead II*, *A Nightmare on Elm Street*, *Silver Bullet*, and *Child's Play*. So when I undertook to write this play, I knew I wanted some element of horror in it. As I wrote, I was reminded of Marie DeFrance's "Bisclavret," which I had read about a year earlier.

"Bisclavret" is a very cool, very short piece about a werewolf written in 12th century France. In the story, the wolf after whom the tale is written would remove his clothes to transform into a werewolf, so his wife took his clothes one night and trapped him in his wolf form. He ultimately repays her by biting off her nose and having the king banish her and her recently-taken lover from the kingdom. After contemplating this baddassery, I knew my play needed to be about a werewolf.

Theater has been one of my life-long passions, and I've dabbled in acting for most of my adult life. I take acting very seriously and put all my energy into every role, rehearsing tirelessly. As a multi-faceted musician, I fixate on a similar process while writing and composing music and have done this consistently since I was ten years old. I put this same drive into writing this play. Once, while taking a break from writing to read an act from *Hamlet*, I laughed at the thought of a Shakespearean character existing today, always speaking to people in iambic pentameter. This thought ultimately led to my protagonist, Boris, and the decision to make the play a dark comedy.

After deciding upon Boris' goals, intentions, quirks, etc., I developed an outline for his story. The other characters in this story were assembled from pieces, like Frankenstein, of people I know or have known, thus bringing my monster to life. On that note, I would like to dedicate this play to the people who helped and inspired me the most: Ethan Gainey, Jellie Quick, Megan Woosley-Goodman, Adam Houle, Landon Houle, Benjamin Hilb, and Jon Tuttle.

I hope you enjoy watching my creation trip over its own shoelaces in this heart-warming tale about family, friends, drugs, and a poet's fear of never being heard.

- Colby Quick

August 2022

Moon Swallower was developed in conjunction with The Jasper Project's Play Right Series in spring and summer, 2022, and received a public, staged reading at the Columbia Music Festival Association on August 28, 2022. Community Producers were Bert Easter, Ed Madden, James Smith, Kirkland Smith, Bill Schmidt, Paul Leo, Eric Tucker, Cindi Boiter, and Wade Sellers.

Moon Swallower was directed by Chad Henderson. Cast and crew were as follows:

Boris Clavel	Michael Hazin
Marie Clavel	Becky Hunter
Peter	Chris Cockrell
Britt	Richard Edward III
April	Lonetta Thompson
TV News Reporter	Chad Henderson
Stage Manager	Katie Leitner
Costumer	Erin Cooper

SETTING:

Marie and Boris's modest home in a rural area.
The stage can be split in two. On one side, Boris's bedroom/Britt's bedroom/Boris and Marie's living room. The other side, Restaurant/Marie and Boris's kitchen. Lights may be used to illuminate one side, leaving the other in darkness.

FEATURED CREEPS:

Boris Clavel: Mid-to-late 20's male

Marie Clavel: Boris's Mother/late 40's, early 50's

Peter: Marie's boyfriend/Pastor/early 50's

Britt: Boris's friend/Pot head/Boris's age

April: Marie's close friend. Marie's age.

TV News Reporter: Male or female.

MOON SWALLOWER
SCENE I

At rise: A young man, Boris, is sitting at a desk in his dimly lit bedroom, typing away on a laptop. He is wearing large headphones and has his back to the audience. He spins his chair around to face the audience and places his headphones around his neck. A cell phone is propped on a stand/tri-pod front-center stage and is recording him.

BORIS.
>A tale to tell that tails behind the mind
>have I, and do I intend to unveil,
>to bring light to dark and sight to the blind—
>clouds of shadowy doubt to soon dispel
>at the expense of false prophets I find.
>Expose naked truth of hair, tooth and nail.
>Steeples sprouted where aimless paths did wind,
>forcing the snail into his lunar shell.
>Lycanthropes knew the ropes before mankind
>ever ascended from dwellings in hell,
>and for centuries trod through shit unshod,
>a fictitious fraud in the eyes of God.
>
>That's right, loyal viewers and Youtubers!
>'Tis I, your favorite humble wolf howling,
>>'how's it going?'
>
>As the sun suppresses the moon's glowing
>I offer my unaltered flesh for uncensored showing.
>Knowing I must—under no circumstances
>>of sound mind—
>impose my nocturnal, beastly instincts
>on the frail joists of society,
>
>I have incorporated elementary techniques
>for keeping the 'dog on its leash.' You see,

> my dealings with mortal humans elongate my
>   elation, whereas
> my moon-lit excursions extend the expanse of my
>   deepest sorrow.
> So! How then do I maintain 'impulse control'?

(Enter, from behind, Boris's mother, Marie Clavel. He does not notice her. He removes ropes and chains from a bedside drawer.)

> To my headboard post, I remain tethered
> with chains and shackles, by day's end fettered.
> I will now demonstrate this for better—

MARIE.

> What are you doing in here, filming porn?

BORIS.

> Mom!

(Boris runs to remove phone from stand and stops the recording.)

MARIE.

> Look, you're grown, and I support whatever you do, so long as it brings you happiness. I just think you wouldn't have to do this kind of thing solo if you'd get out and meet people occasionally.

BORIS.

> My curse is mine to harbor, not to share. Besides, I meet a lot of people online and, within my virtual domain, I am crown-bearer to lost children, banished into hiding by—

MARIE.

> Okay, listen… Honey, I'm proud of you for getting your bachelor's in English but I really wish you would speak to your mother like a normal person. 'Kay?

BORIS.

I did not endeavor to be born, nor did I willingly submit to this affliction to which I am eternally bound!

MARIE.

Well, we'll have to agree to disagree on the latter. Now, come on! I need you to bring the groceries inside.

(Marie exits the room.)

BORIS

(softly:) Her invalidation brings the brothy contents of my bowels to a boil.

MARIE

(voice raised to be heard from off stage:) Families disappoint one another, Hun! It's what we do! Get the groceries!

BORIS

(sighing:) Woe.

(Exit Boris. Lights fade to black/curtain.)

SCENE II

At rise: Boris mopes at the kitchen table while Marie prepares lunch.

MARIE.

Are you okay with me adding garlic to the mashed potatoes?

BORIS.

Why would I care?

MARIE.

Just checking.

BORIS

(deep, annoyed breath:) I'm not a vampire.

MARIE.

That's good to know. *(Pause.)* So... did you pass your test this morning?

(Boris lightly nods, does not look up.)

Good. *(Pause.)* Do you want to talk about it—

(Marie's cell phone rings. She checks her phone then looks over her shoulder to see if Boris is looking. She then ignores the call, putting the phone down/away.)

BORIS.

Was that Peter?

MARIE

(takes a deep, annoyed breath:) Mmhmm.

BORIS.

Why would he be calling you?

MARIE.

I don't know, I didn't answer.

BORIS.

Well, why'd you look over your shoulder at me?

MARIE.

Boris, I am not having this conversation again.

BORIS.

Oh, miserable revelation! Blind me with hot pokers! Puncture my ear drums with ice picks! You said he wasn't your type, what changed?

MARIE.

My mind. I'm sorry to disappoint you.

BORIS.

Since the birth of the Catholic church—

MARIE.

For the last time, he's not a priest, he's a pastor. Don't be ridiculous.

BORIS.

His kind oppresses mine all the same, if not more! I swear by mine eye, in time, justice to restore—

MARIE.

Stop rhyming! Peter isn't oppressing you and I don't have time to stand here and explain to you why you're being crazy… God. I try to be patient with you but you're just so odd sometimes.

BORIS.

At least I'm not shacking up with some Christian! What do you guys even talk about; how great God is at killing everyone?

MARIE.

Hey! You will not speak to me that way in my own house. Do you understand me?

BORIS.

How should I speak to you? Through prayer?

MARIE.

You know what? That's it. Get out.

BORIS.

You used to trust my intuition!

MARIE.

Out!

BORIS.

Why is it different with Peter?

MARIE.

Boris, leave!

BORIS.

> This is what they do! They use their divisive ideologies to turn people on one another! It's all meant to keep us subservient and fearful of knowledge like slaves!

MARIE.

> I don't have time for this.

(She grabs her car keys.)

BORIS.

> Fine. I'll leave for now. It should be easy enough to find a more welcoming spot to loiter.

MARIE.

> Yes, please. Go hang out with one of your little weirdo friends! I'm done cooking and I'm done defending my personal life!

(Boris approaches front-center for a soliloquy. Stage goes dark, except for a spotlight on BORIS.)

BORIS.

> Sick villain, prepare yourself… I will foil whatever nefarious plot you have in store for my mother. Your manipulative charms will fade into abysmal darkness, outshined by the light of truth revealed. I wouldn't be surprised if you were a demon from hell, a minion of Satan himself, ascended from the lake of fire to transform my mother into your mindless succubus.

(Exit Boris. Stage lights return. There's a knock on the door.)

MARIE.

> It's unlocked!

(Enter April.)

Hey. What's up?

APRIL.

Nothing much. Just thought I'd swing by for a bit… Hey, what's up with Boris? He was walking down the driveway when I pulled up. I waved, but he kept his head down the whole time.

MARIE.

Long story, he'll be fine. What's up?

APRIL.

Girl… did you hear about Mrs. Kettman?

MARIE.

No! What happened?

APRIL.

You are not going to believe this. You know that big, gray dog she's always out walking?

MARIE.

You mean the one that's three times her size?

APRIL.

Yep. That's the one… Well, apparently, it went missing sometime last night after she let it out to use the bathroom.

MARIE.

Oh, no. That's terrible.

APRIL.

It gets worse.

(*Pause.*) They say she found it the next morning laying just beyond the tree line in her backyard. Girl… they're saying something ripped that dog to pieces!

MARIE.

Oh my God!

APRIL.

I know.

MARIE.

That's… I mean, how is that even possible? What could have done that?

APRIL.

Girl, you know I don't know. A bear, or something? Maybe a wolf.

MARIE.

Are there bears and wolves around here?

APRIL

(*shrugs:*) I guess so.

MARIE.

Wow… That's so awful. She loved that dog.

APRIL.

She got more exercise out of it than she ever did Mr. Kettman, that's for sure.

(*April chuckles.*)

MARIE.

Maybe I'll give her a call in a little while. Poor thing.

APRIL.

Yea, bless her heart. Maybe I'll make her one of my edible bouquets.

MARIE.

Mm. If she can stand to eat right now.

APRIL.

Everyone's gotta eat. You want to ride with me to the produce stand?

MARIE.

Sure. I'll go grab my coat.

APRIL.

Cool. I'll go warm up the car!

(Exit April. Marie grabs her coat then exits. Lights fade to black/curtain.)

SCENE III

At rise: Boris is sitting on a beanbag chair in Britt's bedroom, silently counting money. Boris finally hands the money to Britt who pockets it without counting.

BORIS.

Thanks again.

BRITT.

No problem. Oh! I almost forgot; did you see how many people have watched the video as of this morning?

BORIS.

I'd rather not talk about it.

BRITT.

What!? Ah, come on, man. You've got to get over that, it's legendary!

BORIS.

So was the Spanish Inquisition.

BRITT.

The what?

BORIS.

Irrelevant. I said I don't want to talk about it.

BRITT.

I feel you, bro. Finish what you were saying before... about the guy who called your mom.

BORIS.

    Right…

    With silver tongue, the devil spreads his lies.
    They crawl like maggots through her ear canal
    and buzz around inside her head like flies,
    spitting acid while sucking on her rationale,
    washing the brain clean, hoodwinking the eyes
    imprisoning will, and draining morale
    until, at last, she so defeatedly cries—

    (Looks to audience:) 'feed me my lines and recite them I shall!'

(Pause.)

BRITT.

    Honestly, bro, your mom's been single for a long ass time now. Your dad died, like, twelve years ago and I don't think I've ever known her to date anyone else. Not trying to overstep or anything; I'm just saying. Maybe you could at least meet the dude and see what he's all about. If he proves to be the son of a bitch you think he is, so be it.

BORIS.

    You know my feelings regarding so called "holy" men.

BRITT.

    I know you feel a lot of ways about a lot of things.

    (Pause.) Look, I'm your best friend. I've always got your back, but it's also my job to be the voice of reason.

BORIS.

    I know.

BRITT.

It's for your own good. I mean, bro, you don't even know what this guy looks like.

BORIS.

That's not true; I've seen his Instagram. He really likes beige shorts.

BRITT.

You know that does change things… Still, you don't know him, like… at all.

BORIS.

I don't want to get to know him. I excel at not knowing people I don't want to.

BRITT.

But I bet it means a lot to your mom, though, right?

(Boris scoffs.)

I'm telling you, bro. You stir up too much shit.

BORIS.

So?

BRITT.

So maybe take it easy for once.

BORIS.

That would be most unbecoming of my true character. Disingenuous.

BRITT.

It's whatever. I'm just saying.

(Boris drops his head back onto the beanbag chair defeatedly, and pauses in contemplation.)

BORIS.

I don't know…

(He lets out a loud sigh.)

Perhaps it is better to go with the flow.

BRITT.

Bet, yo.

BORIS.

Yes, I suppose so… At any rate, I really must go.

BRITT.

Later, bro!

(Britt laughs proudly for successfully maintaining a rhyme scheme with Boris. Exit Boris. Fade to black/curtain.)

SCENE IV

At rise: Marie is dining with Peter in an upscale restaurant. Food and drinks have already been served. Both are well-dressed; they are on a special date. They are both positioned so they're viewed from the side.

PETER.

　Mm... This salmon is fantastic. I can't believe I've never tried it before now. Mmm... Want some?

MARIE.

　Ew, no thank you.

PETER.

　You don't know what you're missing. Seriously, try a small piece.

(He extends his fork toward her face. She stops him by pushing his arm away, avoiding the fork with a disgusted look on her face.)

MARIE.

　No... Have you ever seen a salmon before? They're so... silvery...like someone's filthy pocket change.

PETER.

　Ah, but the color of their meat is so pretty it's named after the fish.

MARIE.

　Gross.

PETER.

　Do you prefer more tropical fish like Mahi-mahi?

MARIE.

Can we please stop talking about fish?

PETER.

Okay. Sorry.

(They both return to eating their meals. Neither looks up nor speaks for at least ten seconds.)

There's actually a reason…

(He begins to feel around in whichever pocket faces the audience.)

I wanted to have dinner with you tonight…

MARIE.

Wait, I'm sorry…

PETER.

What's wrong?

MARIE.

It's just… The truth is, I need to confess something.

(Peter removes his hand from his pocket.)

PETER.

Confess what?

MARIE.

Yea, see, the thing is… I still haven't told Boris about us. *(Pause.)* Look, I'm sorry, I've been meaning to, it's just that—

PETER.

What do you mean, "about us"? What haven't you told him?

MARIE.

Well, anything. He doesn't exactly know we're togeth—

PETER.

(snapping:) Nothing at all?

MARIE.

No, I—

PETER.

We've been dating for a year and a half now! Jesus! He's a grown man, what's the big deal?! What, he can't handle his mommy having interest in another man?! That's sick! Exactly how much control does he have over you?

(Pause. They maintain eye contact. Peter exhales and lowers his shoulders.)

MARIE.

Got that out of your system now?

PETER.

I'm sorry… I was surprised…

MARIE.

Well, he probably suspects something's going on now. He saw me ignore your call earlier.

PETER.

Let's have dinner again tomorrow night, the three of us. Give him a chance to get to know me.

MARIE.

I would like that, but—I'm telling you—Boris wouldn't go

along with it.

PETER.

What? Dinner? Why? When did I ever do anything to him?

MARIE.

You never did anything. He just… has his ways.

PETER.

I don't know who he thinks he is, but "his ways" are a pain in the ass.

MARIE

(*laughs:*) You have no idea.

PETER.

How is this resolved? …Where do we go from here?

MARIE.

Maybe I can convince him, I don't know.

PETER.

He lives under your roof; he shouldn't need convincing! I'll go over there right now and—

MARIE.

Noo!

PETER.

I'm not afraid to be honest with him, you are.

MARIE.

You're going to make things worse, believe me.

PETER.

We won't know until I try.

MARIE.

No, it's okay, I promise. I'll give it a shot when I get home tonight. It'll be better if I talk to him.

PETER.

And if that doesn't work?

MARIE.

Listen, my son's not entirely unreasonable, he's just… eccentric. I'm sure he'll come around… eventually.

PETER.

If not, you can always give me a call. I'll head right over and straighten him out the good old-fashioned way.

MARIE.

I said I'll talk to him.

PETER.

Good.

(They both return to eating their meals in silence, avoiding eye contact. Lights fade to black/curtain.)

SCENE V

At rise: Returning home from dinner, Marie enters her kitchen to find Boris resting his head on his folded arms atop the table.

MARIE.

Hey, I'm home *(Pause.)* Boris?

(Boris lifts his head abruptly. His speech is slurred, and he is visibly intoxicated.)

BORIS.

Oh, hey.

MARIE.

What's the matter with you?

BORIS.

Nothing, just… meditating.

MARIE

(giving a dismissive wave of her hand:) Listen, I need to talk to you about—

BORIS.

Peter?

MARIE.

Yes. Peter. Now don't interrupt me because I have something to say, and you're going to let me say it!

BORIS.

Hmm. Okay.

MARIE.

Peter is a kind man who I care very much about... I've been seeing him for a year and a half now and during that tim—

BORIS.

Holy Shit! A year and half?

(Marie hits Boris hard on the arm.)

MARIE.

Don't interrupt me! ...During that time, I've felt as though I've had no other option but to keep my relationship a secret from you. That's not healthy for me, Peter, or you.

BORIS.

Well... we all must be healthy.

MARIE.

I'm not finished!

(Pause.) If the two of you got to know each other better, I know you could find some common ground. To that effect, I have invited peter over for dinner tomorrow and you will be there. You will be there on time, you will be polite, and you will not embarrass me. Is that understood?

BORIS.

M-mother... I think that would be... reasonable... and it's certainly doable. Although, I don't understand why you feel the need to be s-so demanding. I'll be there.

MARIE.

Seriously?

BORIS.

Yea. No worries.

MARIE.

Okay... That was suspiciously easy.

BORIS.

Your suspicions are unwarranted, I assure you... I understand that you feel as though I m-may be... intruding into your personal life more than what is... customary or expected of a son.

MARIE.

Are you sure you're feeling okay?

(Boris stands up from the table smiling.)

BORIS.

Of course, I... just doing some... internal research.

MARIE.

What the fuck does that even mean? Why are you slurring your words?

(Boris falls over onto the table. Marie gasps and runs to his side with surprised worry.)

Boris! Oh my God, baby!

(Boris stands up quickly, laughing.)

BORIS.

I think I just fell asleep while standing up! I feel great now, though. Weird.

MARIE.

    Jesus Christ, how high are you? B… I thought last time was—

BORIS.

    I'm not high. I'm not s-slurring my words.

MARIE.

    How could you do this?

BORIS.

    I don't know what you mean.

MARIE.

    Bullshit, your pupils are dilated, and you sound like someone tasered your tongue! I can tell when you're on drugs; what was it this time? Please tell me it wasn't pills.

BORIS.

    Wait… dilated pupils and slurred speesh? Oh, no…

(Boris pauses to look at hands as if for the first time. He looks up to the ceiling, becoming focused and steadied.)

    Earth's natural satellite has now waxed to its fullest face. It is time I shed my clothes as the rest of the Lycan race. Join me in crying out to our mother as she splits the day, And—

MARIE.

    Boris, *I* am your mother! And now is not the time for kidding around, you're going to fail your next drug test! Did you forget about parole? Huh?

BORIS.

    Mother, please! We must hurry! Help me to my room so that I may bind m-myself! There isn't… much… time…

(Boris groans continually as Marie speaks.)

MARIE.

    Cut the shit! I'm being serious! My biggest fear is you going to prison for a long time. You never consider my feelings. I have nightmares about it almost every single night. Then I wake up crying.

(Marie sobs. Boris begins pulling at his collar as though he intends to rip his shirt. Boris speaks in growling voice, occasionally snarling, from here on.)

BORIS.

    I'm sorry… but I won't fail my drug test. It wasn't that kind of drug. We really do have to hurry.

MARIE.

    You finally admit it. What was it?

BORIS.

    I don't know. I only know it can't be d-detected in a u-urine test… I asked.

MARIE.

    Oh! Well, I'm glad you're so responsible with your bad decisions!

BORIS.

    I don't have much time!

(He continues his loud cry until able to successfully rip his shirt at least halfway down, if not all the way off.)

Quick, mother! Guide me to my chambers! Make haste! I must be bound! Please, it's for your own pr-protection!

MARIE.

Do you hear yourself? What, are you so out of it you can't find your own room? *(Pause.)* Fine, come on. I'll help you to bed.

(Marie struggles to usher Boris off-stage as he seemingly undergoes 'transformation' spasms. Once off-stage, Boris howls loudly like a wolf. Lights fade to black/curtain. Boris howls again.)

SCENE VI

At rise: lights return. Britt sits in his room eating a bowl of cereal, staring straight ahead at nothing. His phone rings, he checks to see who's calling then answers. Continues to eat cereal as he talks.

BRITT.

Hello? …Sup, Boris? …What? …Wait, you told your mom!? …Well, how did she find out? Did you tell her you got them from me? …Oh, okay. …Oh, shit! You just fell face first? …Woah, really? Last night? …Were you able to get chained up or whatever? …Damn, that sucks about your shirt, though.

(Britt Laughs.)

I would have shit myself… Oh, what were they? Why? You don't like them? I thought they were great. …Well, they're called Moon Drops. … I don't know. They're round and white and look like the moon, I guess. …What? You're where?

(Pauses a moment in confused contemplation. Puts down cereal bowl.)

Yeah, come on in.

(Britt puts away his phone. After a few seconds, Boris enters.)

Sup, bro?

BORIS.

Hey.

BRITT.

Why'd you call if you were already on the way?

BORIS.

It's a long walk. That's a lot of time to worry.

BRITT.

Worry about what?

BORIS.

Will the pills cause me to fail a drug test?

(Pause.)

BRITT.

No way, man. You're golden. That stuff's all-natural. Made from a plant in, like, Bolivia or something.

BORIS.

There are plenty of all-natural drugs that will set off a urine test.

BRITT.

Not this stuff, bro. The guy who sold it to me is a security guard at the power plant. He takes them all the time, gets randomed on the reg, and has never had a problem.

(Boris lets out a loud sigh of relief.)

BORIS.

Oh, good. Mom had me paranoid I'd get locked up again.

BRITT.

Nah, you're safe. When is your next drug test?

BORIS.

They're random. My last one was early yesterday morning.

BRITT.

>Oh, dude, you're fine. The next one probably won't be for, like, two weeks or something. No worries.

BORIS

>*(visibly relaxes:)* Yea, you're probably right.

BRITT.

>No doubt!

BORIS.

>Hey, do you have plans this evening?

BRITT.

>No, why?

BORIS.

>I'd like to, without reservation,
>Extend a dinner invitation
>Might I expect the pleasure be fulfilled?
>Upon acceptance, I would be most thrilled

BRITT.

>You want me to come to your house for dinner?

BORIS.

>Most accurate.

BRITT.

>Like, with you and your mom?

BORIS.

>Yes, and Peter. Peter the pastor.

BRITT.

Ah, dude… You know how awkward that's going to be?

BORIS.

I am aware.

BRITT.

Do you think it'll be a good idea? What if, like, everyone starts fighting or…like…crying?

(Britt cringes at the thought.)

BORIS.

If she's planning on making meatloaf, as is customary of her on Thursdays, I scarcely suspect anyone will be moved to tears unless she adds too many onions again.

BRITT.

Ha! Your mom's meatloaf sucks.

BORIS.

The truth is… I want you there—

BRITT.

Aww, Dude…

BORIS.

To serve as an active buffer between myself and Peter. It was, after all, your suggestion that I get to know "the dude."

BRITT.

That's fair.

(Britt contemplates the offer.)

You know what? I've got you, B. Consider me there.

BORIS.

Thanks. It means a lot.

BRITT.

Seriously, dude, don't sweat it. I know you'd do the same for me.

(Pause.)

BORIS.

Know that I hold your camaraderie dear
and am eternally grateful to you. Sincere
Is my claim that I no longer feel fear.
Clouds have cleared, and—

BRITT.

Boris.

BORIS.

Yes?

BRITT.

Look, I'm going to be there, but you gotta take it easy with the poetry stuff, man. I'm way too high right now.

BORIS.

Oh.

BRITT.

Yea…

BORIS.

    I beg you forgive me...
    I do it habitually...

BRITT.

    Weirdo. You want to watch a movie or something?

BORIS.

Actually, I was hoping you would help me with today's video.

BRITT.

    Right now? What do you need me to do?

(Boris removes his cell phone from his pocket and passes it to Britt)

BORIS.

    I just need you to hold the camera for me. It'll only take a second.

BRITT.

    Ok. Cool.

(Britt holds the phone up to film Boris who pauses to collect himself before speaking.)

BORIS.

    It shall come to pass
    that I will cross paths with a zealot.
    He may have clean piss
    but something's amiss, I can smell it!
    If I can help it,
    I'll learn his secret just to tell it
    and once it gets out,
    mine will be the mouth to propel it!

    Salutations, one and all!

'Tis your trusted changeling come to call.
I'm filled with desperation,
thus, I must make this declaration.

Tonight, a lamb passes the threshold of the wolf's den. On behalf of our kind, I will expose the oppressor for what he is and video every second of it! Then we will prove to the world, once and for all, that we are the real victims! They are the monsters, not us! We will reclaim our place among them, free from exile! No more hiding our true, superior forms from the delicate sensibilities of the brainwashed masses! No more living under the tyranny of the churches! Tonight, we pull wool from over eyes and remove the wicked charlatan's disguise! Stay tuned.

(Pause. To Britt:) Okay, great. Thanks.

(Britt stops the recording and returns Boris's phone to him.)

BRITT.

What was that about piss?

BORIS.

I don't know. I made it up in the heat of the moment.

BRITT.

Hmm. Are you sure you're not getting a little carried away?

BORIS.

Relax. If Peter has nothing to hide, he has nothing to worry about it.

BRITT.

Are you thinking about going wolf?

BORIS.

    The wolf comes when it wants. Thinking isn't a factor. *(Pause.)* Do you still want to watch a movie?

BRITT.

    Yea…. Something light-hearted, though… Maybe even animated.

BORIS.

    Fine by me. I doubt I'll stay long enough to finish it anyway.

BRITT.

    Cool.

(Britt lifts a remote to turn on his TV. A news report, only heard by the audience, begins to play.)

TV NEWS REPORTER.

    …an alarming spike in missing animal reports as authorities continue to investigate what the online community have dubbed the "Full Moon Livestock Massacres." Experts agree the culprit is likely "a large species of—"

(Britt changes the channel.)

BRITT.

    I fuckin' hate the news.

(Lights fade to black/curtain.)

SCENE VII

At rise: Marie and April are sitting together at Marie's kitchen table sharing red velvet cake.

APRIL.

Wow, I can't believe they both agreed. That's crazy.

MARIE.

Yea, well… I think Boris only agreed because he was stoned.

APRIL.

Girl, don't complain, just take it and run!

(They chuckle)

I hope it isn't pills again.

MARIE.

Honestly, April, I don't know what it is. I mean, I can't worry myself to death over this shit anymore.

APRIL.

I don't blame you. You shouldn't.

MARIE.

Right. If he wants to make dumbass decisions, let him.

APRIL.

Does he like pot?

MARIE.

Pot? I don't know… Why?

APRIL.

Well, you remember Jennifer's niece, Deana, right?

(Marie nods in affirmation.)

Girl, she used to be hooked on all kinds of stuff. Her parents had to get her out of trouble so many times it ain't even funny. But then she switched over to pot and gave all the rest of it up just like that.

MARIE.

Isn't pot the worst possible thing for a drug test?

APRIL.

Oh, right… That's so ridiculous. Haven't they proven it cures cancer and shit?

MARIE.

I'm not sure.

APRIL.

It's not even addicting. Remember how much I used to smoke back in college?

MARIE.

Yep.

APRIL.

I quit cold turkey after graduation. No trouble.

MARIE.

Well, Boris's issues aren't with addiction, per se. He just has reckless tendencies.

APRIL.

Ah. Like David, huh?

MARIE.

Exactly like David.

APRIL.

Funny how that works.

MARIE.

Well, it makes perfect sense. They did everything together.

APRIL.

Yeah…

MARIE.

Sometimes I can still see them sitting on the couch, watching old scary movies in the dark. That was their favorite thing to do together.

APRIL.

Oh, I remember the horror movies clearly, girl!

(April and Marie chuckle.)

MARIE.

I never had the nerve to finish one, but Boris always could. Even when he was little.

(Pause.)

APRIL.

I think meeting Peter will be good for BORIS.

MARIE.

I hope so… How are things with you and Richard?

APRIL.

Oh, no. Gross.

MARIE.

What? Why? I thought he was sweet.

APRIL.

Yea but you know how it is. Started feeling a little bit too much like a relationship.

MARIE.

Is that really a bad thing, though?

APRIL.

Oh, the worst. I don't know how you do it. Peter must have a magic dick.

(April and Marie laugh.)

MARIE.

We actually haven't had that much sex lately.

APRIL.

Why? Been too busy for it?

MARIE.

He has been, yea.

APRIL.

Doing what?

MARIE.

I'm not sure exactly. I think he's been focusing on his sermons a little more than usual. He's oddly private about that sort of thing but I know he always gets home late from church now. Not to mention, his second job at the drug st—

APRIL.

Wait, you're not suspicious?

MARIE.

A little.

APRIL.

And you haven't confronted him about it?

MARIE.

I'm not the jealous girlfriend type. Besides, I'm lucky he even puts up with me.

APRIL.

Bullshit. He's lucky to have you.

MARIE.

I don't know about that.

APRIL.

Well, I do.

MARIE.

I mean, who wants to be with a woman whose 28-year-old son still lives at home?

(Marie begins crying. April slides her chair closer to Marie, then consoles her.)

I had a dream the other night…

APRIL.

What was it about?

MARIE

(still sobbing:) I dreamt Boris went to prison again.

APRIL.

Oh, honey, I'm sorry…

MARIE.

That's not the worst part. (*Pause.*) The worst part is…I felt relieved.

(Marie sobs harder. April shushes and consoles her)

I know it was a dream, but it felt so real. I was so happy he was out of the house I didn't care where he was.

APRIL.

It was just a dream. You can't feel guilty for something that didn't happen.

MARIE.

I feel guilty.

APRIL.

Well, stop. You just need space and that's okay. Like you said, he's 28. When you were 18, you had an apartment, went to school, and worked a full-time job.

MARIE.

> That doesn't matter. Boris does things in his own way. I love having him around, I just wish I had more time for myself.

APRIL.

> Hey, I get it. You don't have to convince me.

MARIE.

> I still feel bad. He's my son, I would die if he got into trouble again.

APRIL.

> Relax, he's not going to! He made a mistake once, but he's smart. Don't worry!

MARIE.

> You didn't see him last night. *(Pause.)* I was scared my dream was coming true.

APRIL.

> You shouldn't take your dreams so seriously. Most of them are just metaphors for other things. I think you just need to get laid!

(April and Marie both chuckle.)

> I'm serious! Do something for yourself. You do too much for everyone else.

MARIE.

> Thanks. I might do that.

APRIL.

> Wait, what time is it?

(April pulls out her cell phone and checks the time.)

Shit.

MARIE.

Gotta go?

APRIL.

Yea…I'm sorry, I really didn't mean to stay so long. I've got to stop and get gas before I go to work, or I might not make it!

(April stands up to leave)

MARIE.

That's okay. Thanks for the talk!

APRIL.

Anytime! Listen, text me and let me know how dinner goes.

MARIE.

Will do! Drive safe!

APRIL.

I will. Bye!

(April exits off stage. Lights fade to black/curtain)

SCENE VIII

At rise: Marie is alone, preparing food in her kitchen. Peter walks up to the edge of the stage and stops.

PETER.

 Knock, knock!

MARIE.

 Hey, babe!

PETER.

 Hey there, kitten.

MARIE.

 How was the drive over?

PETER.

 Typical.

MARIE.

 What are you doing? Come in.

(Marie Chuckles. Enter Peter.)

 You don't always have to wait to be invited.

PETER.

 Forgive me. I had an old-fashioned upbringing.

MARIE.

 Yea, yea.

(Peter approaches Marie.)

PETER.

You look hot!

MARIE.

Well, thank you, Mr. Old-Fashioned. I know.

(Marie and Peter kiss.)

PETER.

What's for dinner? Smells great.

MARIE

(trying to be enticing:) Well, I'm cooking some grilled asparagus… Corn on the cob with butter—

PETER.

Ooh!

MARIE.

–and baked… honey… garlic—

(Peter grimaces.)

—chicken!

PETER.

Oh.

MARIE.

Oh?

PETER.

Hmm?

MARIE.

You said 'oh.' What 'oh'?

PETER.

Oh. I don't know.

MARIE.

You meant something, just say it.

PETER.

Well, it's just…I'm allergic to garlic.

MARIE.

Really? How did I not know that?

PETER.

Mm. It's not a problem. It's a mild allergy.

MARIE.

I'm sorry, I didn't even know that was possible.

PETER.

Hey, I'm just happy to be here without having to sneak around!

MARIE.

Shh! Boris will hear you!

(Boris enters.)

BORIS.

I'll hear him what?

MARIE.

Nothing, Hun. Dinner's almost ready.

(Marie looks back to Peter.)

And don't worry, I'll make yours without garlic, it's no trouble. I haven't added it yet anyway.

(Boris looks over at Peter suspiciously upon hearing his mother say this.)

BORIS.

Why don't you like garlic, Peter?

PETER.

Allergic. Are you a garlic fan?

BORIS.

Mm. The biggest.

PETER.

Oh.

(Peter laughs nervously.)

Okay.

(Doorbell rings.)

MARIE.

Who could that be?

BORIS.

It's Britt. I invited him to dinner.

MARIE.

Oh?

(Boris walks off stage. Marie looks to Peter and shrugs.)

PETER.

(speaking low:) Who's Britt?

MARIE.

Boris's friend.

PETER.

(still speaking low:) His friend? I thought the whole point of this dinner was for the three of us to—

(Boris returns with Britt in tow.)

BRITT.

Hi, Ms. Clavel!

MARIE.

Hi, Britt.

BRITT.

(to Peter:) Hey dude. Sup? Name's Britt.

(Britt extends his arm for a fist bump. Peter pretends not to notice.)

PETER.

…Not much.

MARIE.

You all go chat in the living room while I finish up in here. I'll call you when it's ready.

BORIS.

Britt and I can wait at the table.

PETER.

    Ah, come on. A little male bonding never hurt anybody. What do you say, fellas? Join me in the living room?

MARIE.

    (To Boris.) Yea, Hun, go ahead. I can't have you all crowding the kitchen anyway, now go! Shew, shew!

(Marie shews them all off stage. Exit Boris, Peter, and Britt. Lights fade to black/ curtain.)

SCENE IX

At rise: for this scene, Boris's bedroom has been refashioned into a living room with a couch and chair. Britt and Boris are sitting next to one another on the couch. Peter is sitting in the chair. He looks around the room.)

PETER.

Your mom's a great decorator. *(Pause.)* I like what she's done with the—

BORIS.

You're doing a bad job of pretending you've never been here before.

PETER.

What?

BORIS.

Don't insult my intelligence, Peter.

PETER.

That wasn't my intention. I just didn't know you knew.

BORIS.

I didn't know. You just told me.

(Britt laughs but quickly covers his mouth.)

PETER.

Mm. That's clever.

(Pause.)

BRITT.

Yo, Peter. What do you do for a living, man?

PETER.

Well, I have two jobs; I'm a pastor and I work part-time at the drug store.

BRITT.

Oh…

BORIS.

That it?

PETER.

For the moment. Yep.

(Pause. He looks over at Britt.)

Forgive me, I've forgotten your name.

BRITT.

No worries. It's Britt.

PETER.

What do you do for a living, Britt?

BRITT.

Uh, well, nothing really, right now. I mean, I work for myself… I guess I'm somewhat of an entrepreneur.

PETER.

How so?

BRITT.

Oh, you know. I deal… uh, with a lot of, like, the trading of goods… and stuff. Investments, capital, profits, you know. Stuff like that.

PETER.

I see.

BORIS

(to Peter:) So, do you have a passion for preaching and pushing pills part-time? It must be hard to manage expenses on such a modest salary.

PETER.

(visibly restrains his initial retort:) …I do better than you think. It must be hard to meet women while unemployed and living with your mother.

BRITT.

Oh, shit! Below the belt.

BORIS.

I have my reasons for keeping away from women.

PETER.

Oh…

(Peter looks at Britt then back at BORIS.)

Are you two…

BRITT.

(defensively:) NO!

BORIS.

Britt is my closest friend.

BRITT.

Yea, bro. I've got mad honeys on standby, hopping in my inbox wanting a slice of your boy.

PETER.

Well, you never know these days. Everyone's in such a hurry to condemn themselves.

BRITT.

What?

PETER.

I'm just saying.

BRITT.

Dude, my sister's gay. That's not cool.

PETER.

You're the one who got defensive about it.

BRITT.

Yea, but—

BORIS.

Are you homophobic, Peter?

PETER.

(scoffs:) Hey, I've read my bible. A fact's a fact, a sin's a sin, and that's all there is to it.

BORIS.

Why would you choose to form your morals from such a prejudiced mythology?

BRITT.

Is Catholicism considered mythology?

PETER.

No, and I'm Methodist.

BORIS.

I'm educated.

(Peter ignores Boris's remark.)

BRITT.

Wait, so what's the difference between religion and mythology?

BORIS.

Religion is the act of drinking wine
And kneeling before the likeness of a suffering
 deity
But when one claims to have drunk blood divine
That is when one transitions into the realm of
 mythology

BRITT.

Dope.

PETER.

(shaking his head in disapproval:) Hmph.

BORIS.

Have you no retort, Peter?

PETER.

No. I will live forever in Jesus's name. That's all I need.

BORIS.

No one lives forever.

BRITT.

No one except Keith Richards.

MARIE

(calling from off stage:) Okay! Have a seat at the table, everyone! Food's ready!

(Britt exits quickly, as soon as he hears Marie's call. Boris and Peter exit together. Lights fade to black/curtain.)

SCENE X

At rise: everyone takes a seat at the kitchen table. Before sitting, Boris secretly positions a cell phone somewhere in the room so that it is recording the dinner table. Marie circles the table, placing food on everyone's plate. As she's doing so, Britt smiles with hungry anticipation, Peter stares at Britt with judgmental and disapproving undertones, and Boris stares at Peter with contempt and suspicion.

BRITT.

Smells great, Ms. C!

PETER.

And it looks fantastic!

MARIE.

Thank you, thank you.

(Everyone looks to Boris with anticipation.)

BORIS.

...

PETER.

Say, Bor. You know, I could probably help you find a job working in one of the shops up town. My brother's on town coun—

BORIS.

Boris

(Pause.)

PETER.

...I'm sorry?

BORIS.

My name is Boris. You called me 'Bor'. Don't do that again, please.

MARIE.

Boris, that was rude.

(Marie joins everyone at the table.)

BORIS.

One might consider it rude to have such liberties taken with one's name. Even more so when the act is committed by a fresh acquaintance. Do you find that reasonable, Peter?

MARIE.

Boris!

PETER.

No, it's okay. He's right. I... took liberties.

BRITT.

When I was in high school, there were these mean kids that would call me Britney Spears. That sucked.

(Everyone turns to look deadpan at Britt. Pause.)

MARIE.

...Can we please change the subject?

PETER.

Of course, dear.

BORIS.

What would you like to talk about, Peter?

PETER.

Uhm, well... What are your plans for the future?

BORIS.

How far into the future? Death, ultimately.

(Peter laughs.)

PETER.

That's good, I like that.

MARIE.

Boris, stop being a smart ass. You know what he meant.

BORIS.

I have no plans. I've got a vlog on YouTube that a lot of people rely on for survival. It's important work.

PETER.

How do videos help them survive? Survive what?

BORIS.

I teach other lycanthropes how to survive living in a world full of mortal men. Especially the bible-thumping type. No offense.

PETER.

Hmph. No offense taken if you can tell me what the heck a Lycan rope is.

BORIS.

Lycanthrope! Ly-can-thrope!

MARIE

(rolling her eyes:) He means werewolf...

PETER.

So... what you're saying is that you're a werewolf and you teach other werewolves how to do things online?

BORIS.

It's infinitely more than that but yes.

BRITT.

Yo! His YouTube channel is actually totally legit! He's been getting tons of new followers lately! ...Well, I guess that's mostly because of this, like, crazy viral video of him that's been blowing up.

BORIS.

I really don't think they're interested in—

BRITT.

Dude, no way, it was legendary!

PETER.

I'm interested.

BRITT.

See? Ah, dude, it's great! Someone got a video of him running out of the woods at the butt crack of dawn, totally naked!

(Britt and Peter burst into tearful laughter. To Boris:)

Dude, you must've gotten totally trashed the night before!

BORIS.

I wasn't intoxicated. I blacked out and woke up surrounded by trees.

PETER.

Naked, right?

(Peter and Britt burst into laughter again.)

BRITT.

He's practically famous now! Hang on, I'll look it up. You've got to see it.

(Britt pulls out his phone and proceeds to search.)

MARIE.

Britt, I really don't think that's necessary.

(There is a knock at the door.)

Who is that now?

(Marie answers the door. Enter April.)

Oh, hey, what's up?

(April briskly makes her way toward the table, staring intently at Peter with suppressed rage.)

APRIL.

Oh, I'm good, girl. I just thought I'd come and get me a plate.

PETER.

Hello, April.

(He extends his hand. April ignores it.)

APRIL.

Mm.

BRITT.

'Sup, Ap?

APRIL

(to Britt:) Hi.

MARIE

(making her way back to the table:) Well, it's good to have you.

PETER.

The more the merrier.

APRIL.

You would say that.

MARIE.

What do you mean by that?

(Long pause. April glares at Peter, then looks back to Marie.)

APRIL.

Nothing, girl.

MARIE.

Oh… okay. Hey! Remember how you were telling me about Mrs. Kettman?

APRIL.

About her dog? What about it?

MARIE.

I think I know what happened!

APRIL.

What? How?

MARIE.

There was something about it on the news earlier.

PETER.

I think I saw that. About all the pets that were getting killed?

MARIE.

Yea, but did you see the update about the zookeepers?

APRIL.

Zookeepers?

MARIE.

Yep. Check this out. Two wolves escaped from the zoo— our zoo—and the zookeepers failed to report it, so now they've been arrested.

PETER.

Oh my God, that's terrible! I'm glad they were arrested. They knew how dangerous those things were and yet they just let them run all around like no one would ever notice. How stupid can you be? Makes me sick.

MARIE.

So scary…

PETER.

That's just what this town needs. Wolves.

APRIL

(looks to Peter:) You mean more wolves.

PETER.

What's that?

BORIS

(abruptly:) What happens when you eat garlic, Peter?

(Marie drops her fork onto her plate)

MARIE.

I give up…

PETER.

Why are you so concerned about my garlic intake?

BORIS.

Itchiness? Hives? Swelling of the throat and mouth?

PETER.

Hmph. I'm not going to play your games.

BORIS.

I don't play games, reverend.

PETER.

What's with all the religious jabs? Huh? I haven't even been in front of a congregation in four months.

(Displays deep, immediate regret.)

APRIL.

There we go!

MARIE.

What? You didn't tell me that.

PETER.

I was going to Marie, I jus—

MARIE.

Where do you go on Sunday mornings?

BORIS.

Ooh, good question, mom.

APRIL

(reaching to high-five Boris:) Yea, girl. That's a damn good question.

BORIS.

I knew you were a piece of shit the moment I—

PETER.

I'm getting sick of your mouth, you pretentious little junkie!

MARIE.

Peter!

BRITT.

Hey, man. Uncool.

MARIE.

You can't talk to my son like—

PETER.

Well, it's not like it's some big secret! I work at the drug store he broke into, for Christ's sake. Was I not supposed to find out about it? Everyone still talks about it; the way he got caught for being so high he passed out over the counter!

MARIE.

I don't care! This is my house, and you will not talk to my son that way.

PETER.

He's the one—

APRIL.

Tell her about Linda, Peter.

PETER.

(panicked:) What? Who?

MARIE.

Who the fuck is Linda?!

BORIS.

HOOOOOOWL!

Wicked deceiver, you were on a roll!
But the moon's glow casts over your darkness
Like a master detective in the sky,
Watching as your elliptical wings pass.
God have mercy on your quick-fleeting soul!
I will brandish my canines and bark less

So, I recommend transformation nigh,
Before my claws sever your undead ass!

BRITT.

Jesus Christ, man. Chill.

MARIE.

Boris, please don't transform into a werewolf at the table…
I worked hard on this meal.

(She turns to look at Peter:)

Now who the fuck is Linda, Peter?

(Boris removes his shirt.)

BORIS.

Far more treacherous than a Godly man
Is a blood sucker imitating one!
Creature of the night, it is now my plan
To see your status as undead undone.

MARIE.

Boris, what the fuck?

BRITT.

Yea, what are you talking about, dude?

PETER.

Hmph. I knew it. He's high right now!

APRIL

(to Peter:) Why are you still here?

BRITT.

Maybe I should go?

BORIS.

    Admit it, cretin!

(Boris removes his pants.)

MARIE.

    Boris! SIT...DOWN!

(Boris leans over the table and shouts as if in pain. His body twitches. He looks to Peter and speaks in a broken, snarling voice.)

BORIS.

    You are found out! Why further deceive my mother? Shed your disguise, and I will hound you no further!

BRITT.

    I'm going to go...

MARIE.

    Goodbye. Nice to see you, Britt.

(Before leaving, Britt gets Boris's attention so that only he notices, gives a thumb up and mouths the words 'I got you'. Exit Britt.)

BORIS

    (to Peter:) Charlatan!

MARIE.

    Boris, Peter may be a dick but that's all he is.

PETER.

    What?

MARIE.

    Who's Linda, Peter?

APRIL.

You know Linda. Cheryl's daughter, Linda.

MARIE.

Oh, my God... Peter, she's practically Boris's age.

APRIL.

Mmhmm. She's a slut, too.

BORIS

(to Peter:) Coward! Why won't you face me?

PETER.

Very well, Boris. If you wish to take this course of action instead of letting me enjoy my dinner, I will oblige you.

(Peter stands and begins hissing aggressively.)

MARIE.

Oh, Jesus Christ...

APRIL.

More like the devil.

(Boris picks up his chicken and tosses it at Peter.)

BORIS.

Suck garlic, demon!

PETER.

Ah! Oh, we're throwing stuff now?

(Peter picks up silverware and throws it at BORIS.)

Well, chew silver, dog!

(He hisses.)

BORIS.

Ha! Stainless steel!

(Marie stands up.)

MARIE.

Did you just throw silverware at my son!?

APRIL.

Can I please put my hands on this man?

BORIS.

I'll bite your nose off, you dagger-toothed pseudo-cleric!

(Boris swipes at Peter.)

APRIL.

Fuck it.

(She splashes her drink in Peter's face. Boris pushes the table into Peter who then proceeds to storm around the table to shove Boris, who loses his balance and falls back into Marie, knocking her down. Boris and April leap to their feet and frantically try to help Marie up. Peter tries to do the same, but Boris pushes him back.)

BORIS.

That's my mom, motherfucker!

APRIL.

Knock his ass out, Boris. I'll help you.

PETER.

Marie! Oh my God, I'm so—

(Boris punches Peter in the face, knocking him down. He dives on top of Peter and proceeds to pummel him until Marie gets to her feet and tries to pull him off.)

MARIE.

Boris! Stop! Stop!

APRIL.

Let him whoop that piece of shit, girl.

(Marie successfully pulls Boris off Peter.)

MARIE.

Peter, you need to leave!

PETER.

Leave!? It was an accident, MARIE.

MARIE.

Get out!

PETER.

Seriously? You're throwing me out when it's your grown-ass, pill-head son who can't act normal long enough for us to eat a single goddamn—

(Marie slaps Peter in the face. Everyone grows still and silent. Pause. Peter removes a ring box from his pocket.)

PETER.

I can't believe I was planning to ask you to marry me.

BORIS.

What?!

MARIE.

    I can't believe you thought my answer would be anything other than 'fuck no and get the fuck out of my house.' Go marry your little slut, reverend.

PETER.

    Hmph. Fine, maybe I will. This is more than I signed on for anyway. Have a nice life with your little circus, bitch.

(Britt re-enters suddenly, carrying a large stick he's broken in half to form a stake, and screaming as though he were charging into battle. He charges toward Peter.)

BRITT.

    Prepare to die, you blood sucking fuck!

PETER.

    Wait! I'm not a vampire! Stop it! Stop!

(Uncertain of what action to take, Britt stops and stands still with the stake readied for stabbing.)

BORIS.

    I don't care what you are, or what you aren't.
    Leave. Now.

PETER.

    Marie, he can't talk to his elders that way. Are you seriously not going to take charge of this situation?

MARIE.

    If we have to ask you to leave one more time, I'll do a lot worse than slap you.

APRIL.

That goes double for me.

PETER.

(to Boris:) My brother's on town council, you little shit! I'll have you locked away for the rest of your—

(Britt lunges toward Peter again and shouts. Peter eludes the attempted staking and takes off running. Exit Peter. Boris walks over to Marie and hugs her tightly. Marie appears pleasantly surprised)

BORIS.

I'm so sorry, mom. Are you okay?

MARIE.

I'm fine, Hun. He pushes like a little bitch.

(Both laugh.)

That was a bit too much excitement for one night.

BORIS.

It was.

MARIE.

I'm going to go lay down; I can clean up this mess tomorrow.

BORIS.

Don't worry about it, I can take care of it now.

MARIE.

Thank you. I love you.

BORIS.

    I love you too.

APRIL.

    Goodnight, girl. I'll come by in the morning.

(Exit Marie.)

BRITT.

    Yo, April. You know I've got some killer Kush in right now. When are you coming back by the hou—

APRIL.

    Shh! This isn't the time. I've got to go.

(April walks to the door but doesn't leave. Britt walks over to BORIS.)

BRITT.

    Okay, bro?

BORIS.

    Yea, I'm fine.

BRITT.

    You were right; that dude totally sucked. You don't have to say, 'I told you so,' though.

BORIS.

    I told you so.

(Britt and Boris bump fists. Britt leaves to exit and catches up to April at the door.)

APRIL

> *(to Britt, trying to be discreet:)* You said it's some good shit, right? Can I follow you back home?

BRITT.

> No doubt.

(Exit Britt and April. Boris begins picking up the mess around the stage starting with his clothes. He finally remembers the cell phone, retrieves it, stops it from recording and puts it away before leaving the room. Exit BORIS. Lights fade to black/curtain)

SCENE XI

At rise: Boris is laying in his bed asleep. Marie enters and sits down beside him, waking him up.

MARIE.

Are you awake?

BORIS.

I am now.

MARIE.

Sorry…

BORIS.

It's okay.

MARIE.

Did you sleep good?

BORIS.

I did sleep well, thank you.

MARIE.

Hey, so, you know Peter wasn't really a vampire, right? He was just a jerk.

BORIS.

He didn't respect you.

MARIE.

I know… He may as well have been a vampire, I guess… God, why is it so hard for me to find happiness?

BORIS.

You'll find happiness, mom.

MARIE.

You know, ever since… Honey, I still think about your father everyday but—

BORIS.

I'm not worried about that.

MARIE.

Oh… Okay… *(Pause.)* Well, can you at least tell me what you do worry about?

BORIS.

Nothing.

MARIE.

We both know that isn't true…

BORIS.

Well… I hate that I've never published a single poem. I also hate that I'm single and living with my mom. I feel like a cliché.

MARIE

You're a lot of things, Boris, but cliché isn't one of them.

BORIS.

I want to go back to school.

MARIE.

Back to school for what?

BORIS.

I want to get my master's in creative writing.

MARIE.

Well… why don't you apply for the spring semester? What's the hold up? You could get in anywhere you wanted.

BORIS.

I suspect there may no longer be a hold up.

MARIE.

Really? That's good, Hun.

(Marie stands)

You know, you really are great at writing poetry. Then again, you always were good at expressing yourself with words.

(Marie starts to leave but, after walking several feet away, nearly trips over something. She leans down and picks up ropes and chains from off the floor. She looks over her shoulder at Boris then walks away with them. Exit Marie. Boris gets out of bed and gets fully dressed. He places his phone on stand/tripod center stage and sits in his computer chair facing the camera.)

BORIS.

An end to end all that reaches and bends
The fork crawls nearer under rising sun
And I can sense which of its path's dead-ends
As well as I can detect the right one.
No werewolves, churches, vampires, or witches
No headless horsemen on wooden bridges.
Only ink and the art of written word
And my soul, fuming with a poet's curse
Living in fear of never being heard
My passions carried away in a hearse.

It is beyond time I apply myself,
Detoxify, and work on my mental health

Good morning, sweet viewers and Youtubers
'Tis I, your favorite humble wolf howling,
'I will miss you.'
The surface gives way to the turning screw,
Then there is nothing left to do
But to bid you all 'adieu'

(Boris walks over and removes the phone from the stand, turns it off and pockets it. Exit Boris. Finis.)

ABOUT THE AUTHOR

Born, raised, and trapped in the small, rural town of Chesterfield, SC, Colby Quick keeps himself busy as a musician, performer, writer, actor, animator, poet, and father of two—Anakin Joseph and Evelyn "Evie" Marie Quick. He is currently the lead singer and guitarist of a stoner doom rock band called Juggergnome, and one half of the hip hop duo Ski & Beige. Quick graduated from Francis Marion University in 2022 after majoring in English with a minor in creative writing.

www.ingramcontent.com/pod-product-compliance
Lightning Source LLC
Chambersburg PA
CBHW052117110526
44592CB00013B/1645